SHRINK
MONEY
ADVICE

—— By ——

Dr. Henry Joseph Svec

Shrink Money Advice
From Millennials to Boomers – How to Invest Today
by
Dr. Henry Joseph Svec
Publisher: Etrack Inc.

ISBN: 978-0-9684275-2-1

December 2018

Biography: Dr. Henry Joseph Svec received his Ph.D. from Michigan State University in 1988. A clinical psychologist licensed to practice in Michigan and Ontario, Canada, Henry built his small practice to be one of the largest in Southern Ontario, eventually expanding to offices in Windsor, Chatham, Sarnia and London. He has also been a real estate investor for over 40 years, investing in commercial and residential real estate. Currently he lives on a farm in Blenheim, Ontario, with his wife, Mary. He now spends his working time on continued private practice, real estate investing, wealth management, Angel Investing, writing and leading his new tech start-up ExerciseMD.ca.

While investing in Real Estate – Cash Flow properties has been the primary investment vehicle for the family – Henry has also developed skills in other more conventional alternative strategies. During the past 3 years his TFSA portfolio, for example, has earned 80.4% – and currently, during 2018, 29.12% while the TSX is at -5% and the S&P 500 7.91% up to October. These numbers include Dividends paid by those stocks held in the TFSA. You can see that Shrink Money Advice seems to be working for Henry and Mary. In the final chapters you will learn new investment strategies and the names of those stocks that "Harvey" is investing in, which are all strangely similar to those held by Henry. Yes, he takes his own advice, as he did 10 years ago. You can contact him directly here: drsvec@exercisemd.ca

Disclaimer: Review any changes you will make to your financial strategies or investments only after reviewing those with your financial advisor.

In 2007 I completed my first book "The Message-Finding Freedom and Wealth in Your Life". It wasn't a great title, or book cover, and back then (seems like a long time ago) marketing and creating a book was a very different job. I doubt very highly that you have read or even heard of this first book. In the original book, Peter and Samantha – two fictional characters – are unhappy with their life and financial situation and decide to make changes. They are changes anyone could have made some 10 years ago if motivated to do so.

The question and reason for my writing this updated edition is to ask, "What would have happened to your life if you had followed the path of Harvey, Peter and Samantha?"

I'll start by providing you with the story of our couple as it was written some 10 years ago. After that I will use examples from the story and analyze what would have happened to your financial situation if you had done as had Peter and Samantha. In the final section, I'll outline what I would do today, looking to build a financial future to take care of the next 10 years. You may be surprised how times have changed and even how my recommendations to a fictional Peter, Harvey and Samantha would appear today.

Now let's get started with the original story.

INTRODUCTION

Your alarm blares. You'd love to hit the snooze, but you can't. Your head aches already. It's another workday.

You take a peek at the kids to make sure they're getting ready for school. You have ninety minutes to get to the office, but first you have to finish home chores. You have to make lunches, plan dinner, and get the children onto the school bus.

On your drive into work, you start to review your day. First, you'll have to review emails and talk to your staff about the goals for the coming months. Next, you'll probably attend several meetings in which you'll have to answer questions about last month's sales performance.

You'll discuss potential strategies for improvement.

You sigh as you realize that each month is the same—increased expectations, more pressure, and less time to spend on what you value. You feel like you have lost all sense of purpose in your life. You can't remember having true motivation in your job.

The quality of the time you spend with your spouse and children has decreased. You thought that success meant buying everything your family needed or wanted, climbing the corporate ladder, working until retirement, and sacrificing for those around you. But now you look for other meaning in your life. You long to find passion again.

You read self-help books and listen to the opinions of consultants.

They tell you to follow the models of those who have achieved success. Donald Trump, for example, with his popular television show and numerous books, has a wide following of baby boomers who try to imitate the icon. You are advised to buy real estate, to take risks, to be tough on employees and contractors, and to work hard.

Many self-help gurus tell you that they have the answer, the secret to your success.

Just buy their book, follow their advice, and success will shortly follow. You study these millionaires, but you flounder.

In a way, you could say that I am one of those consultants. I have helped hundreds of individuals achieve their personal, family, and financial goals. The important difference between me and others, however, is that I discourage clients and readers from looking to others for models or plans. The secret to your success is contained within your own potential and is created from your own experiences and family histories. Your map to success is different than the map followed by Donald Trump, your neighbour, or your boss. Your inner desires and past must serve as the guide to what can become your outstanding, satisfying future. But there are some things you must do. I did them and now my financial life has changed forever. The rules of investing have not changed despite these unpredictable times. If you follow the rules of my fictional characters as I have I believe you can increase your chances of financial freedom in excess of the 50-50 you would get with a coin flip or having the monkey throw darts at a page of stocks to pick.

Throughout this book I will take you on a journey. We begin with the story of Harvey, Martha, Peter and Samantha, then take up their story 10 years after they embark on their new investment lives. I will help you understand the methods of investing that work regardless of the time, how to diversify those investments, how to start today if you are 18 or 80 years of age. My plan is easy to follow but for some of you tough to do. The question is how financially independent do you want to be?

But before we begin, I ask that you answer the following question:

"If today were your last day on earth, would you be happy with the way you spent your time?" Please remember that one day this will be your truth—it will be your last day. If you want to change, or if you want to take a peek into your possible future, then read on. I look forward to helping you achieve success. If you have the gift of another day, then let's make the most of it.

PART ONE

1

PETER & SAMANTHA

Peter had been married to Samantha for eighteen years. Together they built a respectable life in small-town Canada. They had two cars, secure jobs, a mortgage, aging parents, two children and a dog, numerous friends, and a line of credit.

But they hated going to work. It seemed to sap every bit of energy out of them. There were moments when it all made sense, when they absolutely loved what they were doing, but those moments seemed few and far between. As they sunk into middle age, they found themselves frequently counting the years to retirement.

Peter didn't think it would be like this. He'd worked so hard to become a high school teacher, having gone back to school to increase his grades for teachers college. Samantha, an accountant, also had to work very hard to make partner at the firm where she had been for the past twelve years. Unfortunately, however, tax season didn't allow for much of anything other than working long days (and sometimes nights) with clients who are determined to pay nothing to the government.

They were whiny and demanding, and Samantha was sick of it.

Peter watched each day as the majority of his colleagues at his school left ten minutes after the final bell. He stayed behind to coach—football in the fall, wrestling in the winter, and track in the spring. Coaching, in fact, was the reason he was a teacher, and although he loved to coach he wasn't paid for these efforts. The principal offered a barbecue once a year, and some leniency with an extra day or two off "sick," but that's about it. The student athletes were also getting more demanding. They wanted to be part of a successful team, but few were willing to put in the training hours necessary for such accomplishments. And their parents . . . well, let's not talk about them. If anyone felt that their son or daughter wasn't getting enough playing time, Peter got everything from complaints to insults.

Professionally, both Samantha and Peter were approaching burnout. They had forgotten why they even entered their respective professions. With their children now sixteen and thirteen years old, they were also having problems in the parenting department.

Samantha believed in strict discipline, whereas Peter was more laid back when it came to enforcing the rules. They argued about this on a regular basis, especially now that Mary, their oldest, was driving and dating.

Financially, their life was also a mess. Even though they had a combined income of over $150,000, they had little to show for it with regard to investments. Both had a generous retirement pension from their work, so they never felt the need to save or invest. Each month they pretty much bought what they needed or wanted, putting excessive purchases on the line of credit which now bulged at $83,000—all used for consumer purchases.

As a couple, they had also drifted. They haven't been on a date for years, often going out to dinner with the children or with friends, but never alone. Sex was an occasional happening, usually based on duty rather than desire. Everything in their life seemed to be in a rut.

Sitting on the back porch on a warm summer evening, nursing cups of dark, strong coffee, both Peter and Samantha were silent. They had just returned from the funeral of Samantha's forty-five-year-old cousin, who had been tragically killed in an automobile accident. Still shocked, Peter couldn't help but begin to recognize the death as a wake-up call about the frailty of life.

"I don't get it; she was only forty-five years old. How is that fair?"

Though she spoke it, Samantha seemed to be asking herself the question.

"She was a good mother and wife. She took care of everything for the family. I don't know how Charley is going to go on without her." She was out of tears now, having been drained by the funeral ceremony.

"You never know when your time will come," said Peter.

Both stared silently at the setting summer sun. Peter was particularly struck by the sudden death. But it wasn't grief, necessarily—after all, he had barely known Samantha's cousin. Nonetheless, the event had an incredible effect on the way he saw things.

"We've got to do something, Samantha. I don't want my life to go on like this. I need to make a change. We need to make a change." "Yeah, right! How many times have you said that and then you just go on doing the same old, same old?" Samantha was enraged by Peter's words. She yelled at him as she finally began to cry again. "We have pensions, we have a life here, the kids are in school; we can't go off on a boat and sail the seas or something. What are you talking about?"

"I don't know. All I know is that we've got to do something. It seems like we hardly have the energy to do anything lately. We run around with the kids, taking them to friends, to the mall, buying all this stuff. What does it matter if we're not happy?" Peter asserted, then looked down into his cup. "Life is about doing our duty for the children," Samantha protested. "We made a commitment to them when we brought them into this world. Dammit, we are going to give them the best life possible."

"Yeah, sure. We give them things. We give them what they want. But what are they learning by watching us? Are they learning that once you get married you just exist? That your job should be a chore? That life pretty much sucks most of the time?"

"Peter, this conversation is over," shouted Samantha. "You should have thought of all this eighteen years ago." And with that she stormed back into the house.

But Peter stood fast. It was time to make a change.

2

Their backyard bordered an organic farm that appeared, although it was quite small, to create a comfortable living for Harvey and Martha, their neighbours. The two couples had grown close. Their neighbours were so kind to them, it was hard not to be friends!

Harvey provided the family with healthy vegetables in season, fresh eggs, and the Christmas turkey. While Harvey farmed, Martha ran a local cleaning company. She hired a number of local townsfolk to work in her growing company. Her business cleaned houses and businesses on contract. In fact, it was Martha's crew that came to Peter and Samantha's house once a week to do general cleaning.

But the kind, quiet couple next door had a unique past. For about twenty-five years, Harvey and Martha had both practiced corporate law in Toronto. Very successful in their profession, they had invested their incomes in the stock market, only to see their holdings shrink by 90 percent in the "dot-com" crash. That was their wake-up call.

Harvey loved to garden and Martha had always wanted to start a cleaning business. So they took what was left of their savings, sold their condo in Toronto, and paid cash for the rundown farmhouse and ten acres of land just outside a mid-sized town in Ontario.

In the eight years that Peter had known Harvey, he had rarely seen him unhappy. During the first years of his market garden business, Harvey often got angry when the insects or pests ate into his vegetables.

But gradually, as he got the hang of it, he was able to use natural techniques to maintain a pristine farm. After he conquered that obstacle, he seemed happy most of the time.

He and Martha also appeared to be deeply in love. Although married for just over thirty-five years, Peter would often see them holding hands in town. A couple of times he even saw them kissing—once on the tractor, of all places! They lived modestly, but always appeared to be in the best of moods. They seemed to look forward to their work and life. They took amazing trips in the winter, travelling to Asia and Europe just last year alone.

As Peter sat on the back porch deep in thought, Harvey was getting closer with his cultivator. Peter gave a wave and Harvey stopped his work. He jumped off and walked over to where Peter was seated, coffee in hand.

"Hey neighbour, how goes the battle?" asked Peter.

"Battle? What battle? I'm just out playing tonight. Don't really have a need to cultivate, I just thought I'd get on the tractor and enjoy the night. Martha is at her reading group in town, so it's just me out here, taking it easy. How about you?"

"Just got into it with Samantha a bit. She's upset with me because I'm talking again of switching careers or making some kind of change in our lives. She's upset. She says that it's our duty to stick with it until retirement. I hate going to work, Harvey. I dread Monday morning when I have to drive in. Don't get me wrong—I love working with the kids after school with football and everything, but it's a pretty long day."

"Well, Peter, Samantha is right—you can't make a rash decision when it comes to switching jobs or quitting. You have to plan it through, take your time, and make sure it is the right thing to do."

"Yeah, that is some great advice from a corporate-lawyer-turned farmer! Didn't you make that switch in about three weeks?"

"Not exactly, Peter. Martha and I planned on leaving law for three years before we made the switch. The market crash changed some of our plans, but we were determined to leave corporate law when we did. We had to work on our relationship, our finances, our parenting skills, and even go back and find out more about what our ancestors did for a living. I found out that I had a great-great-grand-father who was quite a farmer back in his day. Seems like he developed some of the organic techniques we still use today. It was a complex task to prepare for this, but it was some experience! Now Martha and I couldn't be happier."

"Where did you find out how to do this?" asked Peter. "I bring it up on a regular basis, we dream a bit, but then we get right back to our old ways of doing things, waiting for retirement."

"The reason it took us three years is because we did it by trial and error until we felt we were ready. We went to accountants, bankers, family and marriage therapists, psychologists, and yes, even lawyers."

We put together a team of advisors to help us make this transition. We didn't have to pay them much, because most of our talks were over coffee. You know, the five-dollar-a-cup kind! We always bought.

Because they were friends, we were very up-front about why we were meeting. They're still friends, and occasionally I send them a basket of vegetables from the farm as part of my thanks to them for helping.

"Both Martha and I were burning out fast as lawyers. Our children were also feeling the pressure, as we had less mental and emotional energy to spend with them. We were there physically, but it seemed that all we were doing was meeting their material needs and wants—shoes, sports, rides, video games, things like that—instead of what really mattered."

"Martha and I were growing farther apart, as well. To tell you the truth, some of the office secretaries were starting to look pretty good to me. That was my wake-up call. I knew that if the blandness of my life was going to lead me to be unfaithful to someone I loved and cared about, I'd better make some changes."

"Martha had her own wake-up call, too. She got on a flight to see a client, but when she got off the plane she found herself in the wrong city! She called me crying from Winnipeg, as her clients waited in Quebec City. So we both were given wake-up calls. The thing is, we listened to the message. Let me repeat—we listened to the message and decided right then to make changes in our lives.

Everyone gets messages, but we often chose not to listen to them. Did you get a message, Peter? What is it this time?"

Peter stopped to think. "Well," he said softly, "Samantha's cousin was just killed in a car accident. I guess that's what got me thinking about my own life."

Peter's kind neighbour probed further. "So, what is the message? What do you think you should be doing?"

But as Peter began to answer, Harvey saw Martha standing by the house in the quickly fading light, waving to him. "Sorry, friend— I'd better get going. It's getting dark and I have to get the tractor back. And Martha is home. It's our foot massage night. She picked up some new oils to try. I'm truly sorry to have to run, but think about what I asked you and we'll talk about it later. Okay?"

With that, he was gone. Peter was more confused than ever. But although he didn't know what to do yet, he was determined to start taking the steps necessary to change his life.

But first, he had to convince Samantha that changes were necessary.

How would he do that? She was so insistent that they must not think about any drastic changes, that their path was already taken, and that they must stick with their current jobs and lives until retirement.

How could he help her recognize that there were other possibilities?

Maybe Harvey could help him. He would ask him to meet for coffee sometime soon. It seemed like his and Samantha's only chance.

3

It was a warm, lightly breezy summer night. The crickets were singing, the starry sky was clear, and it was humid but not hot. It felt like summer should feel. The moon shone strongly and completely above them. It wasn't full, but gave more than enough light to make an evening walk inviting and comfortable.

Peter tentatively held on to Samantha's hand. She was limp and without feeling as they walked. He told her it was going to be a simple coffee chat with neighbours. Four weeks had passed since the funeral, and a different sense of self and purpose had begun to settle inside Peter. He was determined to take control of his life.

They entered their local coffee shop and were immediately welcomed by the sweet smell of freshly baked pastries and strongly brewed coffee. Seated near the window, Martha and Harvey didn't even notice them come in. They were enthralled with each other's every word. As they approached their neighbours, Peter suddenly became very afraid. "Samantha will freak," he thought, "when she finds out that I have shared a number of very personal issues with a neighbour. I told Harvey about everything—our marital problems, our differences when it comes to raising the kids, our financial difficulties. I'm in trouble."

Peter's fears began to disappear as Harvey kindly welcomed them.

"Hey neighbour!" Martha pulled out seats for them both.

"Thanks for meeting with us. I haven't explained the entire purpose of this meeting to Samantha yet. So perhaps you can help me with that," Peter said shyly.

Samantha, looking puzzled, somewhat angrily sat down.

"Is this about changing jobs again, Peter?" she asked sharply.

"Samantha, Peter asked Martha and I to meet with you both and talk about our experiences in switching careers—the steps we took to find happiness and passion in our personal, financial, professional, and spiritual lives. We're not here to convince you of anything, just explain to you what we did to achieve our goals. Would you like us to begin, then?"

"Peter, you could have been honest with me. Jesus, it feels like I've been ambushed here!" She stared down blankly, thought for a moment, and then continued, "but Martha has always been a trusting friend. And the coffee is quite good here. Oh, who cares!—let's get on with it. Peter, you and I will discuss this further when we get home."

Martha began to tell her story.

"When we were living in Toronto, Harvey and I were working very hard at the firm, making lots of money, and feeling pretty much full of ourselves. What more could we have wanted? We had memberships to the country club, the kids were in good private schools, and we had just upsized our home. I was driving a leased Jaguar and Harvey drove a flashy Benz. The children had pretty much everything they wanted too—skating lessons, music lessons, golf memberships—whatever they wanted. We were working fourteen hours a day, but we had a live-in nanny so we didn't feel guilty about leaving the children. I was letting a stranger raise my children and I was okay with it. Now it makes me shudder with embarrassment."

"I was slowly moving up the ladder of achievement. The partners were giving me larger files with unlimited billable hours attached. I think they thought that my child-rearing days were over and so it was safe to invest in me. My day consisted of getting up at five o'clock for a thirty-minute run on the treadmill, then a light breakfast, and finally I was off on the fifty-minute drive to our downtown offices. Harvey would stay a bit longer with the kids, so we drove separately.

He got into work for nine o'clock, but would then stay later. I felt like I was stuck inside a machine."

"I hated my life outside of work. We didn't have any time for vacations, or time alone, so we just kept buying things to fill the gap."

Before we knew it we had over $100,000 on our credit line and were living paycheck to paycheck. We were living in a house worth close to $1 million with a mortgage of $800,000. We were under a lot of pressure.

"Peter, I think Harvey told you of my trip out West. I was to meet a principal owner of a large fish-processing plant who was being sued by the union for unfair practices. I was reading the brief I had prepared, when the stewardess announced that we were about to land at the Winnipeg Airport. At first, I was devastated that I had made such an error. I could have compromised a contract! I was over-wrought with anxiety and shame. But then I began to realize how such an error could have been made."

"I had been living my life on automatic pilot. I couldn't even tell you what the day was like, whether it was cloudy or sunny. I was just existing—just moving. But at least when I called Harvey and began to cry I was feeling something. I was feeling pain, but it was something. For the first time, my emotions were all there. I could feel them swelling inside. That was it. As soon as I got back to Toronto, I handed in my resignation."

Peter and Samantha stared into Martha's strong face. They couldn't believe the determination that such a decision would have taken.

Martha calmly smiled at her husband, who then continued their story.

"When Martha told me she was going to quit, at first I was very angry. I was counting on her income to help pay the bills. Plus, her departure would make the partners question my dedication. At the time, I couldn't understand Martha's reaction to what had happened to her—the children were still young and we had our entire profes-sional lives ahead of us."

"When she got back from Winnipeg, I picked her up at the airport. We had a long dinner at our favourite restaurant on Bloor

Street. As I would later come to realize, that was the first time in years I had seen my wife happy. She was bubbling with ideas. She spoke about how she was going to lay off the hired help, how we could sell the house and buy a condo to cut costs. She also talked of investing in another condo for investment purposes. At the time, I thought she was crazy."

"The next day, one of the senior partners called me into his office and asked me about my future intentions. He indicated that whatever I decided, the firm was behind me. He mentioned consolingly that perhaps Martha was going through some sort of female mid-life crisis. 'Fortunately, men don't have that problem,' he finished."

"I left his office determined to leave too. How could I stay there knowing that I hated the traps I had set for myself, after watching my wife so easily choose to live her life differently? But I had to stick it out for a while. Someone had to bring home a paycheck until we rebuilt some foundations for ourselves."

"We called our best friend, who was also a lawyer at a different firm, and he put us on to an accountant and advisor. We started seeing a psychologist and a marriage and family therapist as well. It was a long three years, but we were able to move out here with their help."

"Financially, we also had to make sure our house was in order. Fortunately, Martha started to buy condos after she left her job. We had four by the time we left Toronto. We still have them and each one kicks off around $1000 in free cash flow per month. It's what we lived on when we started. It's tax-free money—it's like making $100,000 working on salary for someone else. Some people find wealth in their small businesses, stocks, bonds, or other investments. Real estate just seemed to work for us."

"But more importantly, we became financially independent because we learned to enjoy life within our means. We pay off our credit cards every month, and only use credit lines to invest in real estate. We now work because we want to, not because we have to. It makes life a lot more fun. We can explain the details later, if you'd like."

Samantha looked over at Peter and began to shake her head. She was not yet convinced that such dramatic changes were possible for her and Peter.

"But Martha, you are both lawyers! You had a great house and knew lots of people! Plus, you had the money to make this shift. How can Peter and I make a change when we live month-to-month on our salaries and have debt up to our eyeballs? How can we find a team to help us?"

"Your first step is to decide to listen to the message," said Harvey.

"Before you can start looking at a plan with a team you have to be sure that you are going to take the steps needed to change your life. It has to be your number one priority. Once you make that decision, you will have no other option but to move forward. Martha and I would love to help you so that you don't have to make the mistakes we made, or take the amount of time it took us. We could meet biweekly, if you like. How about here, for coffee? The only rule is that you buy. We'll give you homework at each meeting—exercises, things to think about. The work we give you will help you to move forward. It's not about doing anything all of a sudden, it's about planning. Is this something you'd want us to help you with?"

"Of course!" Peter blurted out immediately. Looking over at Samantha, he could see relief in her eyes.

"If it means we will think this through instead of just doing something impulsive, I am all for it." Her reaction surprised Peter. "What is our first assignment?"

"Your first step is to take a yellow pad and write down all of the times in your life when you were given a message. Often these arise from tragic situations—something happens that makes you question your own life. I understand, Samantha, that you recently lost a relative in a car accident. That is an example of a message. You can believe that it happens by random chance, that it is merely a part of nature, or that God or some other higher power is sending you a message. It doesn't matter what you believe the source of such messages to be. Write down each time this has happened to you. We will discuss the importance of such moments on our next visit."

"See you next week, then," said Martha, as she and Harvey lightly headed back into the soft summer night.

4

When Peter and Samantha got home from their first meeting at the coffee shop, they couldn't stop talking. They even made love that night, something they hadn't done in about three months.

What did this talk of taking control of their lives have to do with intimacy?

It was all very strange.

They began their first exercise eagerly and immediately. Peter wrote a list of twelve different times in his adult life when he had gotten a message from some radical change of events or circumstances, times when new possibilities arose and new paths and opportunities presented themselves, times when past ways of living and being were revealed to be unnecessary or even stifling.

Peter became embarrassed with himself as he wondered why he hadn't listened to the repeated messages, like the time his new principal called him a "meathead" in front of other staff. That was a message, one that went unanswered by Peter. Or the time he had to take back groceries while in line at the supermarket. It was the day after payday and he didn't have enough money in his bank account. That too was a message. The death of his mother. The death of his aunt.

These were all messages. And whatever their source, they were sent to Peter and carried the power to lead him to take control of his life and circumstances. Why hadn't he listened to the messages?

Peter became angry. He felt as though he had wasted years. He could feel regret sink into his bones. Why hadn't he listened to the messages? If he had, he would be that much further ahead.

Meanwhile, Samantha was having her own difficulties with the assignment. She was only able to come up with three times when she wondered about her life. Why was she not getting messages? What's more, those few messages she received she had failed to consider fully.

Regret began to set in, much as it did with her husband. Each time such a moment occurred in her life she felt it was her duty to grind it out despite what happened around her. She ignored her messages, too.

The next meeting was at noon on a Wednesday. Samantha and Peter had to struggle to get off at lunch for the meeting. They had asked for an evening meeting, but Martha and Harvey had purposely asked for the noon visit. It was part of their plan.

"Well, how did your week go with the assignment?" asked Martha.

"To be honest, it was very frustrating," said Peter. "I can't believe I've been ignoring these messages all of my life. Why haven't I listened? My life —our life—would be so much better."

"I had trouble, too," cried Samantha. "I don't know! I had a hard time with this assignment. I thought that as adults it was our duty to stick it out no matter how much we hated something. Isn't that what perseverance is?"

Samantha heaved a long sigh as Harvey passed her the napkin dispenser.

"With my cousin's accident, though, I know I need to do something. I'm not happy. And Peter and I are drifting apart."

"The purpose of this exercise," said Harvey, "was to help you see that while you had a number of opportunities to change your lives, you chose not to. Do you know why?"

"Because we didn't know how?" offered Samantha, hesitantly.

"No, that's not quite it."

"Because we're chicken shits?" blurted Peter. He had a habit of swearing when frustrated.

Martha tried to fight off a grin. "Well, I would call it fear, really," she said. "Fear based on a number of factors that we will identify today. Peter, what are you afraid of?"

"I'm afraid that if I leave my job, I'll fail," he answered first. As he thought, more and more fears became clear to him. "I'm afraid that I'll have lost the security of my teaching job. I'm afraid of what others will say if I change. I'm afraid that if I work at our relationship Samantha won't want to work on it with me and I'll get hurt. I'm afraid I won't be able to pay for my children's college educations. I'm afraid of taking a chance. I'm afraid that if I take a good look at our finances, it'll scare the hell out of me."

"Okay. Good. Samantha, what are you afraid of?"

"Pretty much the same things as Peter. I worked hard to make partner and I don't want to throw that all away."

"My message to both of you, then, is don't change anything," smiled Harvey. "Just promise one thing to yourselves and your family: You will never look back and never complain again about your life. You will learn to love it as it is now, and stop dreaming of change, unless you are going to follow through. Frankly, and I can say this from experience, it's not much fun to be around someone who does nothing but moan and complain about their existence. Are you both willing to do that?"

"I'm not," Peter said quickly. "I'm not happy and I'm going to make changes."

"Well, if Peter is going to do this, I am in it with him. Even if it just means better sex, it will be worth it."

Peter blushed. Martha and Harvey smiled. It was starting already.

Soon food would start to taste better. The sky would start to look brighter, more open. Their lives were going to change and there was no turning back.

"Well then, let's move forward," said Harvey. "The reason you're both where you are today is partly due to the experiences of your ancestors and parents. Your genetic makeup, including what your mom faced when she was pregnant, has been proven to have an incredible impact on the behaviours and habits of individuals."

"For example, we know that when women are pregnant and they live through a natural disaster—such as a tornado or a flood—their children are six times more likely to be anxious on the first day of school than children whose mothers did not experience natural disasters while pregnant. Think of it. Everything that your mom experienced while carrying you may have had some impact on who you are today."

"For similar reasons, you also need to find out about your ancestors. What were their lives like? What did they do? Perhaps they were unemployed or poor, perhaps they were uneducated and thought that getting a good job meant salvation?"

"I know about my family," Peter said. "My ancestors came to Canada after World War II. They were refugees living in camps until they came here. My dad was a butler and my mom was a maid. They worked as migrant field labourers as well. All my life they told me to get an education and a good job with the government. As a teenager I didn't listen. But looking back, I guess I did exactly what they wanted me to do. They were right—it did provide security for my family. But if you think of the courage it must have taken my dad and mom to escape to Canada, they sure were risk-takers."

Harvey thoughtfully considered his friend's past, then offered an analysis. "That could be why you were never happy working as a teacher. Part of you, the risk-taking part, wasn't having your needs met. Your mom was also in an uncertain environment while she carried you. That likely contributed to your anxiety and need for security as an adult. These aren't the only things that influence your life, of course. They are merely part of the picture. Still, such histories can be helpful to learn and understand. No one wants to make the mistakes of previous generations all over again! We should want to learn from them."

"Your parents taught you that taking the incredible risk of leaving and escaping to another country was worth it. They also taught you that taking a risk for love was worth it. Wasn't it love that forced them on their uncertain path, the one that eventually led to Canada? I remember you telling me about their romantic connection. Your dad actually left his home in Eastern Europe to escape to marry your mom, right?"

Peter nodded eagerly, moved by newfound admiration for his parents.

Harvey continued. "So, you see? Risk-taking had its rewards for your mother and father. How does that compare to your wanting to risk leaving your job as a teacher?"

"I don't take risks," Peter admitted. "That's why I'm unhappy at work. I don't have freedom. I've got security, but no freedom. The only time I'm free is when I coach. And, of course, I love to coach. I think that I've been afraid to listen to the messages because I didn't want to disappoint my father. But really, he was probably the biggest risk-taker I've ever met."

Samantha's story was somewhat different. She talked of growing up in a home where love was not shown. Samantha's mother thought of work as a duty or responsibility. Jobs weren't supposed to be rewarding or gratifying, but were a duty to a woman's husband and children.

Samantha's mother wasn't allowed to listen to the messages as they came to her. It wasn't her place.

Samantha and Peter looked at each other. For the first time they were beginning to understand why they had chosen their lives. They had done so as if on automatic pilot. It was time to think this through—to make choices based on their innermost wants and desires.

"I have another question," stated Peter. "Why is it that by looking at our lives we are starting to grow together as a couple? We're spending more time together lately. I don't mean just time, I mean real 22 Part 1: Peter and Samantha time—time when we're really listening to each other. Why is that?"

"It's because you are sharing your feelings. You are both vulnerable as you do these exercises, and that will bring you closer together. It's taking you off your traditional path, off of 'autopilot,' so to speak. It will only get better."

"By the way, if you go through all of these exercises and don't change careers, you will still never be the same. You will be working at your jobs because you will choose to, not because you have to. And now for your next assignment."

"We want you both to spend the next two weeks planning what you want your life to look like. You need to identify the goals for your personal, professional, and financial lives. Think about what your spiritual goals are, as well. We will discuss this at our next visit."

"One more thing—the goals must be specific. For example, a financial goal may be to realize a passive income of $100,000 per year within the next three years. A personal goal might be to spend more quality time together, let's say an extra thirty minutes daily. Understand? Try to sketch out your goals as concretely as possible. See you in two weeks."

5

Over the next two weeks, Peter and Samantha thought a great deal about their current task.

Peter had no problem with the assignment. His goal was to work part-time, three days a week. He also knew that he wanted to continue to help children in some capacity—perhaps at a private school or private tutoring enterprise. He also wanted to continue to coach football and become involved somehow in cooking.

Samantha was having a bit more trouble. She loved being an accountant in the sense that she loved to help individuals achieve their business goals. She did get to do a bit of this type of consulting, but generally it was rare in her current practice.

"What would I truly love to do?" she wondered, as their next meeting with the neighbours quickly approached. Finally, on the day before the next coffee meeting, she came up with a plan and goal.

Excitement raced through her body as she wrote down her response:

My goal is to work in my own financial management practice where I help small businesses with tax planning for the future. I will do this for two days each week. I also want to start baking muffins and cookies to perhaps include in a small gift basket business.

When Wednesday night came around, Peter and Samantha arrived early with anticipation. They had printed off their responses to the assignment and were very proud of their work.

When Martha and Harvey arrived, they were in their usual moods.

That is to say, they glowed with jovial exhilaration. Harvey had brought fresh herbs for the coffee shop owner as a gift. And after a bit of friendly chatter—they happily discussed the benefits and difficulties of organic produce—Harvey was ready to get to work.

Martha and Harvey reviewed the homework sheets and sighed, almost in harmony.

"I had a feeling this might happen," said Martha. "You've based all of your goals on your professional life, on what you do. You currently define who you are by what you do. You didn't write any goals for your life as a couple, or as parents, or for your spiritual or financial lives. You need to write goals for each of these and bring them next week. But since you decided to start with your professional lives, we might as well start there. Have you ever wondered how you picked your chosen professions of teaching and accounting?"

"I think I always wanted to help kids," said Peter, a little disappointed that he had so hastily completed the assignment.

"And I was good at math. My father always told me I'd make a great accountant," Samantha revealed.

"So Peter, you became a teacher and a coach because you wanted to help children. Is that how you spend most of your day?" Harvey asked, even though he seemed to know the answer.

"No, most of my day is spent doing paperwork and managing a class of disruptive children. I only get a chance to really work with children when I am coaching. That's likely why I'm not satisfied with my job. As we've already discussed, I also think I picked teaching because it was a secure form of employment. Once they hire you, it's pretty difficult to get fired. It's a great income, too. Plus, I have summers off."

"Have either of you asked your employers what options there are to work part-time," asked Harvey, "or whether or not it's possible to take a leave without pay in order to recharge your batteries?"

Peter and Samantha silently shrugged a "no."

"Peter, check with your union representative. And Samantha, I encourage you to talk with your partners. It is important to see what options you have, should you choose to pursue other avenues."

"Now, today I want to talk to you about how you are using your time on those aspects of your life that you find important. On a piece of paper put down the headings of the different roles you have in life."

Peter, you are a father, husband, teacher, son, and so on. On your paper you should have these as headings along with those parts of your life you haven't developed yet. They can be hobbies or other interests. Each heading represents a part of your life. Make sure you have each part of your life represented; even including future dreams of hobbies or activities. Then think about the amount of time you are spending on each aspect of your life. Not just clock time, but truly invested time, time when you are really focused on that area.

"For example, Peter, when you are with your children, are you focusing on them or thinking of work? Next time we'll talk about how to use this as a guide to moving forward. It will also become the blueprint for your future goals, one for each of your headings."

"The other task is for you to develop your life plan as a couple. If you were both retired, what would you want to be doing at 9:00 A.M. on a Monday morning? You need to be on the same page with this."

"We'll discuss all this on our next visit. But next time, let's do ice cream. I've been drinking too much coffee lately, I think! There's a new shop opening up downtown. It's called 'May's Ice Cream.' See you there next Thursday at eight o'clock."

6

Peter and Samantha found the ice cream shop tucked into a back alley of a downtown street. Although it seemed to be hidden away, Peter and Samantha found the shop to be bustling with activity.

The lineup for ice cream, in fact, was out the door. Peter noticed that Harvey and Martha had already reserved a table. They squeezed through the busy entranceway to join them.

This time, however, their neighbours were not alone. Sitting with them in the ice cream parlour was an elderly gentleman, possibly in his seventies, happily working away at eating a strawberry sundae.

"Hello, Peter and Samantha. This is Bill Mays. He's the owner of this shop and I wanted you both to meet him," said Harvey as he welcomed the couple, who in turn shook Bill's old, warm hands. "He started this shop about a month ago after retiring from thirty-five years of public service at the post office. He always had a dream of opening his own business. Bill knows a little of why we meet weekly.

He's a good friend and he has agreed to tell you his story. I think you might find it to be helpful."

The old man slowly finished the final spoonfuls of the frozen treat, which he found all the more pleasing since opening his own store. He loved to watch others eat, too—such are the pleasures of the sweets vendor! As he happily pushed aside the empty dish, he began to tell his story.

"Friends, I started working for the post office after I got laid off at the plant. That was in about 1963. I was young and strong, but the economy at the time was a bit scary—"

"Bill, why don't you start at the beginning?"

The old man started again.

"My dad left us when I was four years old, and we were always poor. My mom did her best and we had enough food and everything, but kids used to laugh at my clothes and we didn't have enough money for me to play hockey. In a Canadian town that is pretty much a death knell for the social life of a fourteen-year-old! I started to work at an early age so that I could bring home money to help Mom."

"When the post office job came along I took it because I was sick of being laid off. It was all about surviving, but underneath I always wanted to own my own ice cream shop. I have one good memory of my dad. Just before he told my mom he was leaving, he took us all to the bake shop in town, which also made their own ice cream. It was vanilla, and I remember the cone. Even today when I eat vanilla I get a warm feeling all over me. It was the last bit of security I would feel for quite some time."

"I was a letter sorter for the post office. They were long days, but sometimes I'd just dream of owning my own ice cream shop. Funny thing—I waited thirty-five years, and when I was finally retired to a full government pension, I didn't know what to do! I was sixty-five years old and it took me five years to get the strength to give this a try. I am so damn happy. I don't care if I sell any ice cream—I simply love being here in the shop. I love creating new flavours and talking with customers. It's a passion, something I've wanted to do my whole life.

"Peter told me he has talked to you about messages. I can't tell you how many times I received a jolt that got me thinking about my life."

You see, I was numbed by work. This numb feeling was so bad that my wife left too, when our son was three years of age. Luckily, I vowed at the time to stay in his life. He's all grown up now and has 28 Part 1: Peter and Samantha a family. He's working for the post office. Ha! Practically took my place.

"If I'd listened to the messages, many things in my life would have been different. I might still be married. It wasn't her or I that was the problem, it was the way I was choosing to live my life, and the way those choices affected our ability to have a relationship."

"But you know, this past year when I've been planning this shop and then opening it has been the greatest, and I mean greatest, time in my life. I've even started dating again! My friend and I, we're set to go travelling in the winter when we shut down. I'm finally living my life. I'm closer to my son and grandson. I've got a new hobby of fly fishing—I can even tie my own flies now. Life is so damned amazing, I just can't believe I let about sixty-nine years go by before I decided to live. Thank God I've got some time left."

"It doesn't matter what you choose to do, just make sure it is truly your choice. Get rid of the outside stuff, and if you have a dream— go for it. It will change your life forever."

"Well, I've got to go help out at the counter; it seems the line is getting bigger. If I don't give a hand, they'll be backed up all the way to the post office! But thanks for listening to my story. And go ahead and order whatever you'd like—it's on me. It's your first time here. For all new customers, the first cone is on the house. And by the way, in my opinion our raspberry-vanilla is one of the more interesting ice cream flavours this side of the forty-ninth parallel! Give it a try!"

Peter and Samantha stared at each other. What was that? They were sad, yet happy for Bill. It was sad that he waited so long to find his life, but lucky he had the time to go for it. They both knew at that instant that they couldn't wait thirty more years.

"So, how did the assignment go?" asked Harvey, instantly forcing them back into their own situation.

Peter went over their new life plan. "Each day in retirement we will have the opportunity to pursue our own personal and joint goals. For Samantha, she wants to work one day a week in her own tax planning practice. She'll do most of the work online from home, but rent space as needed from her firm. The flexibility of her situation will mean she'll be able to travel any time she chooses. I want to run football camps for kids and start a private tutoring business. I know there is lots of competition out there, but I also want to work one day a week in retirement—the same day that Samantha works."

"We want to have $100,000 in passive income so that we don't have to work unless we want to. We want to spend time with our children. I want to keep up with my hobbies as well. I don't know how we'll be able to do this, but that's our goal. We want to be more in love with each other than we are today. We want to take the time together, and apart, to work on our relationship. We are going to take classes. We're going to a spa in three weeks for a four-day seminar series on enhancing relationships. It's about intimacy, sure, but also about having better . . . sex. We want a better, fuller life together."

"Sounds like you're really taking hold of your lives. How did you make out with the other exercise?" asked Martha.

Samantha began this time. "I came up with a full page and needed extra space."

Her headings were as follows:

So, each heading needs to be given adequate time and attention.

Peter's headings were as follows:

"That's just great, both of you," said Harvey. "You've really

husband	wife
father	mother
son	daughter
brother	sister
friend	friend
spiritual	professional
professional	spiritual
hobbies - cooking	hobby - travel
hobbies - fishing	hobby - writing
hobbies - travel	hobby - future?
hobbies - future	travel

thought about the exercise. Other than your life plan, this exercise gives you the automatic goals you will meet in each area. Your goal is simply to work on those headings each day. Your relationships with family, your spouse, and children should be a daily event. You can't focus all of your energy on your fishing, for example! And you can't focus all of your time on work. You need to be specific in this exercise—fill in the amount of time you will dedicate each day to those areas. Friends may be a more occasional happening, but make sure you set time aside to work on this area too. Also, make sure to take time to travel. Finally, set aside time for your own personal hobbies. Then, when you are both together, your relationship will feel rejuvenated."

"Speaking of relationships, how are you getting along as a couple?" asked Martha.

"We talk every night after work. When the kids are sleeping we sit out back and just talk. We seem to be getting closer together every day. We are really talking and communicating. We're learning something new about each other every day," Samantha said, reaching for her husband's hand.

"Harvey," said Peter, "I've got to ask. What is the lesson from Bill's story? Is it that we shouldn't wait till we retire to pursue our dreams?"

"Actually, Peter, the lesson is whatever you take from it. Remember how he said his son also works for the post office now? Well, he also runs a successful landscaping company in town. And his wife helps out here in the ice cream shop. They travel, invest, and appear to be living their passions. You can have a regular job working for someone else, or even some big organization, and still find your life's passion."

This is what I've been trying to hammer home with all our talk of 'the message.' It's about what is right for you. You can't follow someone else's plan, just your own.

"Okay, maybe we should summarize what we've been doing at our meetings. As a high school teacher of mine once said, 'To summarize is to memorize.' So let's look at what we've learned so far."

"First, we all get messages or awakenings that tell us to perhaps change something about our lives. Rarely do we listen. This is because of fear, previous learning, and the experience of our ancestors. Second, listening to the message means taking on the fear headon and deciding to make changes. Third, the setting of life goals—not only career goals, but also personal, family, and financial goals—is an incredibly important step."

"Finally, identifying each role we play in life helps us set goals for each specific area. You need to be very specific in identifying the amount of time you will spend each day, or each week, on those areas."

"Now, the exercise for this week is about money and wealth. It's about your definition of money. I want each of you to answer the following question: What is money? We'll take this one on next week. How about we meet at our house? We'll cook dinner and then we'll have our visit. Does six o'clock next Sunday night work? Alright, see you then."

7

Samantha and Peter didn't want to do this latest exercise. They usually avoided talking about money because it always led to a fight. They had seemingly incompatible ways of spending and thinking about money.

Peter liked to spend. He had a retirement pension that would take care of them upon retirement, so he saw no need to save. Their house was increasing in value each year—wasn't that an investment?

Samantha was the saver. She reviewed all credit card purchases once a month, which would inevitably lead to arguments. "Did you really need to buy this?" was her common complaint.

Their disagreements about money ran deeper yet—they also led to deception. Samantha had her own private bank account of which Peter was unaware. The account had in excess of $25,000 in it, money which Samantha didn't want to share with Peter. It was her money—why should she give it to him? So he could buy some stupid toy or just squander it?

It was a beautiful fall Sunday when the couples were to meet again for lunch. Harvey and Martha were regular church-goers, so the lunch was the ending of a perfect morning for them. Harvey wasn't particularly religious, but he loved to sit in the church and listen to the calm. He hadn't been active in any religion as a child. He was a "freelancer" of sorts, who loved to go to different churches on Sunday or Saturday—Catholic, Anglican, Islamic, Buddhist, and Jewish, to name a few. He found beauty and peace in them all.

Martha, on the other hand, was brought up Catholic, but she wasn't practicing on a regular basis.

Despite the progress they had made over the past couple of months, Peter and Samantha felt timid and guarded when they walked up their neighbours' driveway. They didn't want to talk about money. Sex would have been easier to discuss.

Before they reached the front door it opened, releasing the sweet smell of roast beef, potatoes, onions, and a freshly baked cake. The delicious food, and Harvey, wearing an old apron with "Tip the Chef!" written in bold, invited them in. He immediately took their jackets.

"Welcome, friends! Martha will be down in a minute. Can I offer you some wine? Red or white? I just received my latest shipment from France—a wine club I belong to sends me a different bottle each month. It's all moderately priced wine for under twenty dollars, but it's very good."

"A glass of red would be great," said Samantha.

"Me too," agreed Peter.

"Sounds great. I'll pour the wine. You can both grab a chair in the den. We'll talk a bit before lunch. That way we can enjoy dinner after getting this tough topic over with."

As Martha finally joined the group, Harvey began the discussion.

"Before we start with your homework today, it might be a good idea to help you both relax a bit. What if Martha and I talk about our relationship with money when we were working in Toronto, and how it's changed since we moved out here? Martha, do you want to start? Remember how you used to worry so much about our finances?"

"Sure, Harvey. Our money situation was a mess in Toronto. We were each pulling in over $200,000 a year, but we were each spending more than that! It was crazy. There were no limits. As we moved up the ladder at work, we kept buying bigger houses and moving into more expensive neighbourhoods. It got to the point where we would be happy with a house, but because we felt like we were in some sort of race, every time we moved we had the smallest house in that neighbourhood."

We couldn't afford the lifestyle of the neighbours, but we tried. In the end, we had an $800,000 mortgage on a house worth about $1 million.

"We had an accountant who kept telling us that we were fine, we had lots of income, and it would continue to go up. He had us work with a financial advisor whom he had recommended. This advisor had us in some dot-com stocks and hedge funds. We lost about $700,000 when that bubble burst. I remember driving home from work when I got the call. They wanted me to put more money in our investment account because of a 'margin call.' I didn't even know what that was, but apparently we had signed papers giving the broker the permission to buy or sell whatever he wanted from our account. We didn't see him but once a year, and thought things were being taken care of. Boy, were we wrong."

"Our credit cards were all maxed out, too. I was paying the minimum because we didn't have any money left after paying for private school tuition, taxes, and all those car payments. Our car payments alone were in excess of $3000 a month."

"As I've said before, in Toronto we were both on automatic pilot. Our lives were controlled by work and the desire to work hard to pay for things. At that time, money was like water or oxygen to a living being. We just had to have it or it seemed like we would die."

"I thought that money was the most important thing in life for happiness. I learned that growing up. My parents were always commenting on how happy their rich friends seemed to be. Don't get me wrong—our situation wasn't my parents' fault. It was our fault, as we chose to follow that path. It's just interesting to notice how our relationship with money as adults has been shaped by our earlier experiences."

"I honestly believed at that time that if we had more money, our relationship with each other and even our children would have been that much better. If you had asked me about my values, I would have protested that the most important thing in my life is family. But I wasn't living my life in a way that was consistent with those values. It was very messed up, to say the least."

"I should also emphasize that it wasn't just Toronto that was the source of our problems, of course! I'm a firm believer that anyone can be happy anywhere, if they make the choice to be. But the particular way of living we were caught up with in Toronto was not healthy for us. And so we needed to make a change."

"So how did you get out of that frame of mind?" asked Samantha.

"I listened to the message," said Martha. "I listened to the message I received in Winnipeg. We'll talk about specifics after lunch, but first listen to Harvey's story while I go stir the gravy."

"Of course, my story is much the same as Martha's. I was very proud of making partner at the practice. It meant lots of money, great lunches on someone else's tab, and acceptance by my peers. I was spending money like there was no tomorrow. I believed, however, that money was an elusive byproduct of success and was fleeting, so you had better use it before it disappears. At the same time, I believed that money was a sign of success. The more of it you have, the more successful you are. I was obsessed with this concept. The problem is that once I got the money I had no clue what to do with it. We would give it to advisors, buy crazy things, and spoil our children. We had no plan for what to do with our increasing income, and that caused a ton of problems. Near the end, we argued about money almost every other day. It was hell."

"Just before Martha quit the practice, we had started to talk to different financial advisors. We finally found someone that was a professional and we paid her by the hour, with no commission on what we bought or anything. She sat us down and we started to take control of our future."

"It's important to remember that when you talk to a professional, lawyer, accountant, or anyone giving you advice—including us—it is just advice. You hire them for their opinion and then you, not the advisor, decide what's best for you. If someone is telling you to buy or sell something, or take a specific action, remind them that you simply want their opinion. You want the best opinion available, sure, but it is you two who will make the final decision.

"When we sat down we learned that we weren't as bad off as we thought. If we sold our house we could have about $100,000 left over, we had $250,000 left in investments, and about $200,000 in funds that the practice owed us. So we started on a simple path.

Martha and I sold the house and bought an affordable condo in an up-and-coming neighbourhood. We put the kids in public schools and cancelled all of our memberships. We took the cars back and bought an affordable used car. Martha started studying real estate as well, and we bought three more condos and then a house to rent out.

"We still have them today and the income from those homes is basically what we live on as we grow our businesses. We bring in $5000 a month in positive cash flow, but there is no tax because we can depreciate the buildings. On top of that they go up in value by an average of 4 percent a year. So, given that our properties are worth about $1.5 million, we are also making about $60,000 in equity each year. It may not sound like a lot to some, but we are actually saving money. We used to spend this much on credit card bills each month, and now we live on it. But we feel like we are wealthier and more in control than we did in Toronto. We take a bunch of trips in the winter and drive great cars. Our house is paid off and we own our life. There is nothing that I feel I need as far as money or possessions go."

"What is very rewarding is our ability to give back. It's not just meeting with couples like yourselves—we currently meet with two other couples in similar situations—but we have a charity fund of $5000 a year where we give to whatever charity we feel at the time."

Last week we gave a check for $1000 to the homeless shelter. We tell them not to bother sending us requests for more, because if they do we won't send them another penny. It's our money and we'll decide how to give it away and don't want to be solicited on a regular basis.

"There are other ways we like to give back—little things. I like to go to Timmy's and give a twenty for a coffee, but tell the hostess to use the change to buy coffee for everyone behind me in line until it runs out. I then leave before anyone can notice what I've done. Can you imagine standing in line for a coffee, tired and needing a jolt of java, only to find out that a stranger has bought you a coffee? How can you not have a better day, be happier, feel that mankind in general is generous? How can you not then be nicer to your spouse, children, or customers? It's a lot of fun and it is one of the gifts that money can give you. Giving back. We stopped donating to churches. We don't appreciate the way they use the money. We had better not go down that road!"

"I would say, though, that the most important thing we had to do was to agree on the definition of money. We had different definitions in Toronto and we were each following a path based on that definition."

Our current definition is: "Money is an important part of life. It is necessary to live, to give back, and to secure our future." We will always have total control over how our money is invested and spent.

We have the power and ability to be wealthy and choose to do so. It will give us the opportunity to give back to others, enjoy ourselves, and compliment our relationships. Our money comes primarily from passive investments that we control. We will continue to grow our businesses and real estate investments so that we realize $100,000 of after-tax income per year. We will build our net worth to in excess of $5 million.

"We both agreed to this just before we moved out here. It's funny; once you and your spouse come to an agreement on a definition, the 38 Part 1: Peter and Samantha fighting stops. Money is no longer the driving force in your life. I can say that setting goals is also very important. Once we did that we surprisingly began to move closer to the goals each month. Because we can live on our income stream from real estate rentals we have no pressure on us. We've decided to take control of our money and spending."

"Okay, it's time to eat. I hope you're hungry! We can talk about your homework over dessert."

8

They barely spoke as they slowly finished the delicious and wholesome meal. The dishes themselves were nothing out of the ordinary, but they'd been prepared with such attention and care that each tasted unique and special. In fact, Peter and Samantha hadn't had such a good homemade meal in quite some time. After they all helped to clear the table, Martha brought out the cake, which she served with a pint of May's homemade ice cream. As they began to eat this sweet finale, they continued their discussion.

"Ok, Samantha, let's hear your definition," asked Martha.

Samantha looked up as her eyes swelled with tears. She had a confession to make.

"I am sorry, Peter, but I've got to tell you . . . I haven't been honest about our money situation. About five years ago, I started a separate bank account and started saving money without telling you. I was afraid of what would happen to us. I was afraid that someday you might ask for a divorce and then I'd be on the street. I've saved close to $25,000 in that account. I am very sorry. Please forgive me."

Peter was at first quite happy. $25,000 in a bank accountant! How could they spend that? But anger quickly overwhelmed him.

"How could you keep that from me? All those months we struggled to make payments—and you had money just sitting there! And you didn't say anything! How am I supposed to trust you when it comes to money now?"

"Now hold on, Peter—don't be quick to judge," Harvey stepped in.

"Did you ever have a time when you bought something that you didn't need, and chose to not tell Samantha?"

"Well, yes, there were times. But not $25,000 worth!"

"Okay, okay. But it's about time you both come clean with your money secrets. It's partly what is stopping you from growing in your relationship. Let's start by having you both agree to be honest to each other in all aspects of your money lives. Do you both agree to this?"

"Well, we can try," muttered Peter cynically.

"I'm sorry, Peter!" pleaded Samantha. She was visibly moved and full of regret. "But I did it for both of us! I was going to tell you, honest. It's just that I was just worried about our relationship."

Peter took a moment to reflect on what they were discussing. All of a sudden, a question came upon him. "Hold on—does that mean that if I choose to buy a coffee I'm supposed to call Samantha and ask for her permission?"

"No! Of course not," piped in Martha. "You're an adult. We're talking about major financial decisions to buy or to invest. You'll have a plan shortly that you will both agree to. Samantha, tell us your story about money."

"I grew up in a house where money was something we rarely had. It was a surprise when we had enough to buy things like birthday presents or special foods. I can only remember going out for dinner a couple of times in my childhood. We couldn't do any of that. My parents worked very hard. They said to me many times that money was something you saved because it was necessary for life. They also said that the secret to making money was to work very hard. The harder you work the more money you would make. They also said that they suspected that rich people were somehow dishonest, which seemed like a contradiction! It was impossible for anyone to make millions of dollars unless they took advantage of others. Money was something you needed, but too much was a sign of dishonesty."

"Wow," she said, "my past likely has a lot to do with why I was feeling very guilty about that secret bank account. It wasn't just that I was keeping the information from you, Peter. It's also because as the amount grew I felt more and more guilty about it. I was feeling dishonest on so many levels. I am sorry. Boy, I feel horrible."

"I am sorry too, Samantha," said Harvey. "But everything is going to be okay. Let's just move on with this. Peter, tell us your money story."

"As you both know," said Peter, "my family was pretty much lowermiddle-class growing up. Money was something you had to use to pay bills, but you never knew when it would be gone. My parents said that we should spend it as we got it, because otherwise it might be gone tomorrow. My dad had a pension from work so he didn't think he needed to save or invest. I guess I was feeling the same way."

"I didn't know there were so many different definitions of money out there. I didn't understand why no one else has the same definition of money as I do. At work they always talk of our pension plan, how if we hang in there we'll be taken care of by the union. What is scary is that the other day I heard that the average teacher only lives two years after retirement. That is a frightening statistic! I'm not sure how true that is, but it makes you think. Harvey, is there a right and wrong definition of money?"

"Actually, Peter, the right definition is the one that is right for both of you. What is important for happiness is that you are both consistent with your goals and definition of money. You do need to take control of this."

We have a number of books for you to read. You should try to read one book on money or investing each month. You both need to increase your 'money IQ.' We will also talk about getting your advisory team together as you move forward with your plans. At our next visit we'll also talk a bit more about real estate, but just because it has worked for us. Please remember, we are not suggesting that you follow our path. You may feel that buying stocks, bonds, or a small business or franchise is the right way for you. We'll just tell you the details of how we got started and how we built our advisory team.

"In the meantime, we want you both to work on your joint definition of money to share with us next time. Be honest with each other, share your fears, and work through the money demons of your past. This is not your parents' fault. You have choice and control. It's time you began to exercise that power. Now, let's have some more of this beautiful cake."

9

Peter and Samantha were confused. Did this mean that they were to leave their jobs and start businesses? It all seemed like too much. Peter brought up their hesitancy at the next meeting.

"I don't want to sound like a wimp, Harvey, but I'm afraid to leave my job and start a business," admitted Peter. "I have a pension and job security."

"Wait a minute, Peter. Remember when we started? I said you would have to find and build your own plan. You can stay working where you are, but if it is your choice then going to work won't be a chore anymore. This exercise is about examining your options and then making choices. Once you make those choices, you will be free."

"You mean I can just keep everything the same, do the exercises, and my life will be better?"

"Well, not exactly. But you can have the same job, the same career, and your life will still change. Let me explain.

"Going to work for the same employer each day has its benefits. You've already talked about the pension you'll get when you retire and about the security of the job. But with security comes a lack of freedom. If you read one of the books I recommend called Rich Dad Poor Dad, the author says that the most security you can have is to be in a maximum security prison. Everything is taken care of for you—food, lodging, and entertainment. But it is not a place we want to be! That is why many of us going to work each day talk about feeling like we're in a prison. So with all the benefits come costs, mainly the cost of loss of freedom. Income is also capped when you work for someone else under salary. Peter, when you help one of your students go on to university and stay in school despite his troubles, do you get a bonus from society? Of course not. You make the same whether you're an amazing, successful teacher or someone who doesn't care.

It's the price of security.

"Now, to own your own business you will have to understand that there are uncertainties. You're never sure when the phone will ring and someone will want your product or service. You'll have to take care of your own retirement planning and health care, but there are certainly advantages if you set up your business the right way. That is why we recommend that you first read The E-Myth, a book about working on, and not in, your business. Our accountant recommended it. It helped us understand that if we weren't careful we'd be just creating another job for ourselves instead of a business that we could control. We would be technicians, not business owners. Technicians are those who work to make widgets themselves, instead of hiring others to use a system to build them. You need to leverage your experience and business ideas.

"Don't get me wrong, I still love working on the farm, and occasionally Martha will go in and help clean an office or home, but we do these things because we want to, not because we have to. The freedom to choose makes all the difference in the world.. Knowing your options, both within your job and with other business ideas, is the first great step to moving forward. You both have many choices; you just haven't looked at them.

"Part of where you are today is because of a number of factors that we have already discussed—your early experiences as a child, what you watched your parents do, and what you listened to. Now it's time to take a critical look at your lives and decide on your own. Take back control over your life."

10

Peter finally spoke with his union representative. He learned that there were many options to work three days a week starting in September. He'd have to pay 33 percent of his benefits and pension plan, but the school board would likely be happy to accommodate his wishes to save money and hire a fresh new teacher out of school to work his extra two days. It would mean somewhat of a decrease in income, but Peter would be able to continue to coach football. The school board also offered a leave-without-pay option, where he could choose not to work for up to two years without pay, to do whatever he wanted. His job would be guaranteed should he want to return after this time period. Peter had interesting options to consider.

Samantha had even more luck with her partners. They were very open to any flexible work options that she wanted to propose. Right off the bat they offered her the option to work from home for up to two days a week, and if she liked she could also take a leave in total from the practice.

Such inquiries are important because the one thing that is needed to enjoy life, regardless of goals or ambitions, is time. No one has more than twenty-four hours a day. How we spend it is our choice, so finding a balance between work and our other pursuits is a key to happiness.

Next, Samantha and Peter looked at their financial situation. With Samantha's stash of money they were basically at zero for their credit cards. After deducting all other outstanding bills they had about $6,000 in cash and $60,000 in RRSPs. Their mortgage on the house was still at $120,000, with monthly payments of $1,200 including taxes and insurance. They also had $20,000 in the kids' college fund.

Samantha had about $40,000 in the practice in the form of retained earnings that she could take out as a dividend.

Their RRSPs were invested in mutual funds and hadn't gone up or down much in the past ten years. Finally, their credit line was maxed out at 7.5 percent interest, and it was used to purchase consumable goods, not investments or anything like that.

On their next visit with Martha and Harvey, both Peter and Samantha were extremely excited. They hadn't changed anything yet, but were brimming with energy and ideas. Peter was convinced he'd take the partial leave option to work on his cooking skills and to set up his tutoring company. He had no clue how to set up a business, he just knew he wanted to do that. He didn't even know if there was a market for his services.

Samantha had sent a letter to the partners indicating she was willing to come to the office one day a week and then work two days from home. It was all very intimidating—their combined income would now be only three-quarters of their current income—but it would give them a chance to take control of their lives with a safety net below them. After all, they still had to pay the bills.

But what had really changed was their relationship. They spent more time talking, but now they seemed to be really listening to each other. It was as though their energy was endless. They also began exercising. At first it was just walking, but progressed to a regular regime of cardiovascular activity before dinner. They both found that their thinking was much better if they exercised. Everything was looking up.

When they got to their coffee shop they were surprised to notice that Martha and Harvey hadn't arrived yet. Usually their neighbours were the first ones there. They took their table and waited patiently.

Peter ordered two cups of the day's special blend. Between the two of them, it tasted of hickory, nuts, and a bit of a good chardonnay!

They laughed and joked. How is it that they could each taste something different in the same batch of coffee? Their playful chatter was interrupted by the waitress, who handed them a note.

Dear Peter and Samantha:

We won't be coming to meet with you tonight. We decided to take a quick impromptu trip to wine country and take in a bike tour and wine tasting. We'll be back in two or three days.

Go ahead and order some fresh pie. We arranged to pay the tab this time. We knew you'd understand and likely not mind, given how both of you have moved forward with your work. One thing you'll find as your priorities change is that you will also take such trips or make such decisions because it is the right thing to do.

Hope you enjoy the private chat together. We'll see you in a week's time. Same bat-time . . . same bat-channel.

Yours,
Harvey and Martha

Peter and Samantha both smiled, remembering the Batman show they had watched as children. They continued their light discussion.

They stayed for two hours, enjoying the pie and each other's company.

When they got home that night, they made love for over an hour.

It was very different. They talked, shared their wishes and desires, told each other what they liked and didn't like. It was as if they had no secrets. Sharing their dreams and wishes had made them more attractive to each other. They couldn't remember ever being this passionate.

It was like a new beginning.

The next week passed by quickly, but Peter and Samantha were in no hurry to meet with their neighbours. They were moving forward with their plans and beginning to feel in control. They had worked out a budget, too. They were looking at savings of $1500 a month after meeting all of their obligations. Plus, they wanted to have a fund for vacations and dates and continue to put money in the children's college fund. They hadn't budgeted anything for new business investments yet, but they were very pleased that they were taking control of their lives. They also had written their own unique definition of money that they both agreed to:

Money is a way to provide us with freedom. It is a way we can be sure to meet our daily obligations, but it is also needed to provide us with choice on how we give back to society. Our goal is to realize an annual income of $150,000 dollars within three years, including passive income of $50,000 per year (although we're not sure what passive income means yet!). We want to have assets in excess of $4 million and successful businesses that feed our passions.

They left the house to meet up with Martha and Harvey at the local park. It was a beautiful night, with crickets chirping and the smell of coffee suddenly in the air. Martha had brought some coffees and stillwarm chocolate chip cookies from the shop.

"Ever wonder why eating chocolate chip cookies make us feel so special?" asked Martha. "It's because it's connected to so many memories of our lives. Good times. Safe and secure times, perhaps when we were children. When you take a bite and eat the cookies, let yourself feel whatever it is that happens."

They all silently focused on the exercise. Frankly, Peter was unimpressed at first—he thought it some sort of Oprah exercise! He was surprised, however, that as he slowed down his chewing he was aware of many of the flavours of the cookie. He tasted the chocolate, a touch of brown sugar, and oatmeal. It did bring on a very calming feeling, and the coffee was also full of layers of flavours. As they all discussed their impressions of the food and drink, Harvey spoke up.

"When we lived in Toronto, I had a coffee and muffin every morning on my way to work. I couldn't tell you what the coffee or the muffin tasted like. As I've said before, I was on automatic pilot. It wasn't until we moved here that I really began to enjoy these types of exercises. Martha reminds me on a regular basis to slow down when I eat so that I can enjoy the flavours. It really is different now. And remember—a love and passion for food is supposedly closely linked to passion and sex. Or at least that's what the shrinks say!

"Before we talk about your money goals, we wanted to talk to you both about passive income. Please remember that you should not follow our plan just because it worked for us. Your plan will likely be different.

You may choose to use stocks that pay dividends, bonds, or mutual funds.

"Passive income is like having a bank machine that gives you money on a regular basis, except you don't even have to go pick it up. It's put directly into your bank accounts.

"We use real estate because we understand it. If you were to buy a property for say, $100,000, and keep it for twenty years, but after that time period it was only worth $80,000, would that be a great investment?"

"No, it would be horrible," guessed Samantha.

"That would be a loss of $20,000," chimed in Peter.

"You both sound like my old investment advisor! Well, actually you are both wrong. It would be a great investment. Let me show you how.

"Let's say that you buy the property for $100,000 and put very little of your own money into the purchase. Say you put $10,000 down and finance the rest. You rent it out and are able to have a positive cash flow of $100 a month after all expenses, and a reserve fund as well. You take the $100 a month and simply put it in a bank account to pay yourself back for the $10,000 you invested. The return on your $10,000, by the way, is 12 percent, which is a very good rate of return. It's tax free as well because you can deduct 4 percent of the 50 Part 1: Peter and Samantha house value every year against any income earned. That means you pay no taxes on the money earned, up to about $3600. In twenty years the tenants have paid off your mortgage. Each year rents go up a bit, so in ten years you are bringing in $250 a month in income after expenses.

"But here is the fun thing—in twenty years the mortgage is paid off. You owe nothing to the bank and now have $1400 a month in income, because there are no more payments to the bank. You can, however, refinance the property and take out say, $60,000 tax-free, continuing to collect the monthly income, minus expenses. So you see—the $80,000 that the property is worth is all profit to you, taxfree.

You also continue to earn passive income, which is the difference between the costs and rent collected.

"Now before you get too excited, it's not all fun and games. At first you may have to manage your own properties as Martha and I did.

From plugged toilets in the middle of the night, to hot water heaters leaking on Thanksgiving Day—we've had to deal with just about every kind of inconvenience. But once you get a few properties, you can hire a property manager to take care of this for you. They charge anywhere from 4–8 percent of rents collected, but then they have all the headaches. That's what Martha and I do now.

"We have three condos and one house in Toronto that now bring us in excess of $5000 a month of profits. That's how we do it. We also have automatic payments to ourselves each month, something you should both do. We have $250 a month going into our 'vacation'

account, and we pay ourselves $500 a month as well in our own 'personal project' account. We put $1000 into savings each month and the rest we use for daily living costs.

"This system works for us. When it's time to go on vacation, the money is there. And when I want to try a new hybrid fruit or vegetable, or when I want to advertise in the local paper to sell my fall produce, I have the money there.

"We are starting to make a profit in our businesses. Martha is now up to four employees. She rarely cleans anymore—she mostly manages the staff. She's even bought a new software program to help manage the schedule. The business income is now over $20,000 a month and growing. We're very excited."

"Wow! From a cleaning business?" gasped Peter. "I'm sorry, but I find that hard to believe."

"Well, it's true," said Martha. "Also, we only work with clients who we enjoy as customers. We have the luxury of choosing who we work with. It's part of my freedom of choice motto. It's also very strange that the more positive we are and the more selective with our clients, the more we bill. But it's true. We're becoming a boutique cleaning company. It's a lot of fun. I also discovered that the less time I spend cleaning and the more time working with staff and market-ing, the more money we make. I've got a great book for you both to read that helped me understand how this is possible."

Next, Peter and Samantha, brimming with confidence, shared their plan.

"Gosh," exclaimed Harvey, after hearing the goals established by their students. "Good for both of you. The fact that you have a strategy to move forward with your plan is also very encouraging. Before we pull the plug, though, let's talk a bit about the establish-ment of your advisory team.

"Martha and I are pretty much finished with what we can offer you," admitted Harvey. They were all a bit regretful that their time together seemed to be coming to an end, but Peter and Samantha glowed with optimism. "It's time you both build the team that will help you achieve your goals. I have a list of three professionals that you may want to interview. You'll need an accountant, financial advisor, lawyer, real estate agent, and insurance agent. That is, if you want to invest in real estate. We've also provided the list of books you both should read to get you started. I also recommend that you consider working with a personal coach or psychologist for the next twelve months to make sure that your new behaviours become habits. I've got some names for you there as well. Remember, you want to inter-view them first to make sure you feel you will be able to work together.

Your final assignment is then to come back in two weeks and talk to us about your team of advisors. We'll do dinner—it will be our last meeting."

11

Before their meetings ended, Peter and Samantha wanted to talk to their neighbours about their differences in raising the children.

They read the books that Harvey and Martha had recommended, but continued to struggle with their differing opinions. The inconsistencies were obvious to the children, who would go to Peter for one answer and then to Samantha for a different answer. A few helpful phone conversations with Harvey set Peter and Samantha back on track.

To start, they learned to put the children on an allowance. They would pay each child their age each week. Each child would then place a third of the money into savings, take a third for daily purchases, and give a third to charity. They were also going to post the following rules:

They must respect each other, and respect each other's personal space.

They must do their best at school.

They must complete, on a weekly basis, tasks which are not included in the allowance list (for free), and tasks that need to be completed to receive the allowance. If those tasks aren't completed then they must be completed with parental support or encouragement, and no allowance is paid for that week.

Discipline was also an issue. It was agreed that grounding would be utilized as a punishment for most behaviour problems. But most importantly, both Peter and Samantha would be consistent and communicate their different opinions on discipline in private—never in front of the children. They also agreed on a strategy to deal with behaviour, which included the following guidelines: After an incident, send the child to their room for five minutes to cool down. This gives the parent an opportunity to think through the punishment strategy.

When the child returns from her/his room, give them up to five minutes to discuss what happened.

Ask the child what they should do next time.

Provide the suggested solution and the consequence.

As a rule, when the discussion is over, it is over.

Both parents should try to have the punishment over within the day. Also, it should be logical in nature. They both agreed to gradually provide more freedom to the children so that by their last year in high school there would be very few rules. This would give Peter and Samantha an opportunity to watch their child prior to moving on to university. They agreed to be a team.

When they implemented this program, it was at first very difficult.

The children didn't think they were serious. But gradually they began to realize that their parents were together on it. Within a month, things settled and the house seemed much more organized. The children spent more quality time not only with Peter and Samantha, but with each other. The plan was working.

12

Harvey was driving back from making his deliveries when he passed Peter and Samantha's home. He was startled to see two police cruisers parked in the driveway. Harvey quickly pulled a u-turn and parked behind one of the cruisers. When he knocked, the door opened slightly. He could see Samantha crying, as one of the officers tried to console her. When she saw Harvey, she ran towards him and hugged him tightly. "It's Peter!" she cried. "He was hit when he was driving home from work. He's dead!"

13

Peter felt light as a feather, a bit like he had way back in grade nine when he skipped his first class. Today he told his school's principal that he was going through a complex dental procedure that required him to leave work for two Monday afternoons a month.

When the principal asked him what sort of treatment it was that he'd be undergoing, Peter just shrugged his shoulders and said, "It's complex."

Of course, he didn't need a note—the principal trusted and believed him. Nonetheless, his dentist was an old buddy from school who had agreed to give him an alibi, if needed.

Samantha and Peter had planned to meet for lunch at a restaurant outside of town. They were working on their relationship. They planned to eat together at the charming, countryside spot, then drive to the larger city nearby and rent a room. They would enjoy themselves, have amazing sex, and return back to work the next day. It would be the second time they had done this. Peter was very excited.

A supply teacher had been arranged to cover his class and there was no football practice on Mondays. It all seemed to work out perfectly.

"Strange that adults sometimes have to lie and make up stories to get out of school or work!" Peter said to himself as he pulled onto the highway.

There was a turn in the road just before the intersection he was pulling onto. He eased onto the highway, and that's when he saw it.

A truck was in his lane, passing a tractor loaded with hay. It was too late. Peter couldn't swerve, couldn't avoid the impact. He died almost instantly.

Upon impact he felt like he was swimming in the lake. He felt a buzzing but no pain. Then, as he drifted above the accident scene, a warm calm washed over him. He could see the driver of the truck get out and start to scream. He could see the tractor pull over and both men desperately try to get his body out of the vehicle. But it was too late. They could only stand by helplessly as they watched Peter's car burn down to nothing.

When the police and firefighters arrived, Peter actually knew a couple of the men who had come to help him. He curled with one of them. He had coached another in high school. After they did what little they could to help, both men sat on the curb and began to cry.

Peter then left the scene. He was pulled away. All of a sudden, he could see his mother, who had passed some years earlier. He felt an indescribable but inviting feeling. "Strange," he thought. "So this is what death is like." It was 12:22 P.M.

At the moment that Peter's vehicle collided with the oncoming truck, Samantha shuddered violently. She was on her way to the restaurant, anticipating a wonderful afternoon and evening with her husband. The sharp chill she felt surprised her, because it was quite warm outside and in the car. She looked at her watch and thought of Peter. "12:20. I wonder what he's doing right this minute. Can't wait to see him."

She waited for over an hour at the restaurant. When Peter still hadn't arrived, she went to the school to look for him. Something must have gone wrong. The school secretary told her that he had left early that day for a dental appointment. Then, taking a different route home than the usual, she saw what was left of Peter's car. "Oh my God," she cried. "It's Peter."

The police tried to comfort her, but they knew Peter as well and were having a hard time holding back their own emotions. They drove her home.

The next days and weeks were a blur to Samantha. They closed the school for the funeral and asked that he lie on the football field so that the team and school could have a service. Many players and former players spoke. Samantha was very touched by the speeches and marvelled at how her husband had helped so many.

At the cemetery a group of players were there in uniform, and provided a sort of honour guard for Peter. It was all very touching.

The police said that the truck driver admitted to being at fault. She had received six calls from different lawyers both in and out of province who wanted to sue the trucking company. Vultures, all of them. Bastards. She worked on helping the children. They cried. The youngest wanted to sleep with her, and she consented. The oldest slept on the floor. She brought in cots and made it a sort of camping event. They were afraid to go anywhere—to travel, to be left alone. Samantha sought out assistance through the school, and the children were referred to a child psychologist in a private practice who understood what children go through when they lose a parent. It was very difficult work, but helpful to the children. Samantha didn't have time to think of herself. It was all about taking care of business, the children, finances, everything. She was left alone to comfort and fend for her children. Aside from the day of Peter's death, she didn't cry much.

14

Twelve weeks had gone by since the accident and funeral. Harvey and Martha had tried to help, but Samantha was very strong and stoic. She took care of all of the funeral arrangements. She consoled the children by herself. She took charge and had things pretty much in order when she agreed to meet for dinner. She was still going to move forward with her plans to work part-time, especially now that she was a single parent. Her children were the most important thing in her life—she had to make sure she was there for them.

Financially, she was better off than she had expected. There was life insurance that paid off all of the debts and left $150,000 in cash. She also would start to receive half of Peter's pension immediately, as well as Canada Pension payments. The children would also be receiving some money from the government.

All this made for a very difficult meeting. Martha and Harvey both cried when they saw Samantha. She had lost weight and looked like she hadn't slept in weeks.

"Thanks for meeting with us, Samantha. We just wanted to spend some time with you. It's not necessary to continue with our lessons.

We consider you a very dear friend. And as we've said many times since the accident, we're here for you."

"Thanks, but I want to continue. Even though I'm a widow now I need to move forward with the plans that Peter and I had worked out. I regret very much all of the time we wasted before we met you both. But I want to thank you for giving us the time to really fall in love again. He was coming home early the day of the accident. We had set up a date where we would eat at a very romantic restaurant and then get a room. He had his classes covered and—," Samantha welled up in tears. "He was very much looking forward to part-time teaching and working on his company and coaching. But we did have an amazing six months while we were meeting with you. We could have lived together for thirty more years and not had the time we did with each other just this past while. Thank you both again."

"But there's . . . something else," she paused, hesitantly. "When I received his personal effects from the school, I found a bill from a credit card company that he hadn't told me about. He had taken it out five years ago and was using it until just after we started to meet.

It had a debt of $25,000 on it. I also found purchases from jewelry and lingerie shops some six months ago. I know he wasn't buying it for me.

"But you know, it all stopped—the spending, I mean—just after we started meeting with you both. And he was paying it off slowly. I don't know if I should be angry or relieved. I don't know what to say. . . . He was having an affair! Peter was having a goddam affair while I was working my ass off at the practice!" Her submerged resentment and anger exploded into rage. "Okay, so it stopped perhaps six months ago, but it still hurts. The bastard! Why did he have to die? I feel guilty because I want to hit him, yell at him, love him . . . Oh God, I am so confused."

"Samantha, I think you should talk to a professional who can help you through this. You've been through a lot and a trusted professional could help."

"You mean a psychologist?" asked Samantha. "I don't need a shrink. I need a husband to help me with the kids, to help me and be there when I come home at night, to make love to me. I don't need a goddam shrink!" Samantha's emotions were flowing—anger resentment, anger disbelief, discomfort, all blended into one moment. She would regret what she said next.

"Fuck the both of you. Living in your hairy-fairy world where I'm supposed to eat chocolate chip cookies like I'm having an orgasm or something. Fuck the both of you. You don't know what it's like. You have each other. All those years of appreciating each other. We had six months. Just go take a flying fuck. You lawyers are all alike."

And with that, she stormed out of the restaurant.

15

It took her eight months to get the courage to call. She had stormed out of the restaurant to drink a bottle of wine by herself at home. She cried for three days. She had spent so much time worried about everyone else that she had forgotten about herself. She finally took their advice and started seeing a psychologist who could help her with the grieving process.

The psychologist told Samantha that because of the suspected affair, she was experiencing an adverse grief reaction to the loss of Peter. Her anger and resentment were stopping her from grieving.

He also told her that each one of us moved through grieving at our own pace. We never completely get over a loss or death—we move on and forward, incorporating that person's spirit into our lives.

Samantha was able to gradually accept the death of Peter and move forward with her life. She would dream of him at times, and sometimes she felt his spirit around her. She couldn't identify it exactly—it was just a sense of calm, a sense of comfort. She was moving forward.

The meeting was to be held at the best restaurant in town.

Samantha insisted on being the host, so she arrived early. The table was private and was set in the back of the lavish establishment. She ordered a fine wine early, giving the expensive bottle time to breathe.

When Martha and Harvey finally got there, they rushed up to give Samantha a consoling hug.

"I am so sorry!" Samantha apologized. "I was completely out of line. I have nothing but thanks to give the both of you—for giving Peter and I a life before he died. I am so sorry."

"Samantha, don't even think of it. We understand that you were going through an incredibly difficult time in your life. We're just happy that you wanted to meet with us."

Samantha called over the waiter and gave her a twenty dollar bill.

"This is for you. Please don't come back and ask for our orders until I ask you to. We have a lot of catching up to do!"

The waitress smiled and left the room.

"First, I want to take this opportunity to share with both of you how my life has changed because of what you have taught me. When Peter died, I spent most of my time recovering and trying to take care of everyone else. I started with the kids and got them help, then Peter's parents. They were so upset. All they kept repeating was that parents are supposed to die before their children. Comforting them was terribly difficult.

"Next, I had to look at our finances. Thanks to the both of you, we were already moving forward. We had started saving, and with the insurance money I have been able to get us out of debt and take care of things. I've got $150,000 in cash that I've used as collateral to buy my real estate properties."

"Properties?" asked Martha, pleased. "Tell us how you did that."

"Well, I looked at the list of books you suggested and just started reading. I read two a week. I had nothing else to do when the kids were at school and it helped me to stop thinking of Peter's death. I started looking at the papers. I also spent some time with Mildred Jones, the bank manager in town. Peter had coached their children.

She was very helpful—she got me started with a line of credit and also advised me as to who I should get on my team. I also began talking with Robert Smith, a local real estate agent who came highly recommended.

I understand he works with the both of you, as well.

"Anyways, my first property was a small condo close to the school.

It was a one bedroom that was for sale for $125,000. The mortgage was $75,000 and I asked the owner if they would take a second mortgage at zero percent of $20,000 for the remainder for five years. I bought it for $95,000. They agreed and I told them I'd fly them to the West Coast to see their children, which is where they were moving to anyway. I took over the mortgage. My total payments are $680 a month. I got a great rate at the bank. I have been able to rent it out for $930 plus, so I'm making $250 a month in free cash flow.

"And I've got six other properties now. I was buying them as I found them, without being concerned about anything once I listened to my advisors. My current monthly cash flow after expenses is $3000, and my goal is to get to $10,000 a month. I've got my money in a GIC as a security blanket, but my assets are growing daily. I've decided this is the best thing for me to do.

"I've got an accountant, as well. The old firm in town brought on a new associate—we had coffee and I can work with her. She is amazing.

"I've also found a lawyer who specializes in real estate, and who I can trust. His rates are reasonable and he has already referred me one deal that we close on next month.

"I've decided to hold off on starting my private tax practice. I've taken a two-year leave from the firm because I think I need time to soak in what is going on now. And the children are moving forward but still seeing their psychologists. That has been very helpful. Thank you again for the suggestion. But boy, was it ever an experience trying to find the right therapist!

"I started by asking around. No one I talked to had any ideas. I just started looking in the online phone book. Then I started interviewing them. One worked out of his basement in his house. I wasn't comfortable with that. Another worked out of his office up at the college.

I didn't think that was right for me either. So I chose to drive the sixty kilometres out of town to a regular full-time clinic with reception and great-looking office space. I'm glad I did that.

"I have to admit that I am still working with this psychologist to this day. The practice there has a personal coaching program and

I've enrolled in that as well. I had only known what therapy was like because of what I had seen on The Sopranos and Fraser and The Bob Newhart Show. But my experience working with a psychologist was very different. He had very high tech office capabilities, with computers and testing. I learned to do self-hypnosis and other techniques to help with stress and to visualize success.

"My spiritual life is also changing. I'm not going to church now or anything, but I am spending time on the water, just sitting and meditating.

I'm also giving back to various charities of choice. I've set aside a fund for this purpose. I'm feeling totally content with my life, with the exception being that I continue to crave Peter's company, love, and support. God, how I miss him. "So to both of you—I want to say thank you so much. I am so sorry for what I said when you suggested I needed help. You helped Peter and I live each day as if it would be our last. His last day was full of anticipation as he headed out to the restaurant for our romantic lunch. Without the both of you we wouldn't have had those incredible six months."

"You are so, so welcome, Samantha," said Martha. "Harvey and I have been very touched by knowing the both of you."

Tears streaming down their faces, they had a big group hug. With that, Samantha summoned the waitress. They ate, drank lots of wine, and closed the place down (they took a cab home, of course). They agreed to meet on a monthly basis to talk and support each other in personal and business endeavors. That night Samantha slept soundly for the first time since Peter's death.

16

I t was the last pile of things to give away to the Salvation Army—
old shirts and some socks and sandals. There were two boxes in the
closet with old papers and letters, too. As Samantha worked through
the boxes she could see a wrapped rectangular box covered with
red paper. Quietly she began to work on the wrappings, and slowly
opened the packing paper. Inside was a black negligee with a gold
and diamond chain. He had made those credit card purchases for
her. Inside the box was a card. She read:

> Dearest Samantha,
>   You are the most important person in my
> life. I am so sorry that I took you for granted and
> I want to start over with you. Our first meeting
> with Martha and Harvey taught me that we need
> to work on our relationship. Please accept these
> gifts as a sign of my commitment to move for-
> ward in our relationship. I love you so much.
>
> Your loving husband,
> Peter

As she tossed the letter to the floor, Samantha finally let out
the screams that she had been holding in for close to a year now. She
cried herself to sleep, holding the gifts in her hand.

17

It had been six years since Peter's death. Martha and Harvey continued to prosper in their business, personal, and professional lives. Martha now had twelve employees and worked only ten hours a week. Her business was netting $500,000 a year and she spent most of her time on the things she loved to do. She met frequently with new and old customers to improve her services. She had hired a bookkeeper and the other supports needed for her to step back.

Harvey, too, flourished on his organic farm. He was beginning to specialize in edible flowers and various types of beans. He was now shipping his produce around the country via overnight courier and he was very proud of his operation's growth. He was netting $40,000 dollars a year and loving every minute of it.

They had grown their real estate holdings to realize free cash flow of $13,000 per month. The value of their properties had increased to more than $5 million. They were only working because they wanted to, not because they had to.

Samantha was also prospering in her business life and her life with the children. She continued to expand her real estate holdings and was realizing a monthly cash flow of $11,000 per month. She wasn't able to move on with dating, but instead she spent her time travelling and with her children. She was working only five hours a week, as she had an excellent property manager to look after the properties. Of course, there was still a significant gap in her life, one that would never be replaced.

It was only now, some six years after the accident, that she was able to fully grieve the loss. She cried daily and was deeply depressed, but with the help of her therapist she was able to finally work through it.

It started after her youngest left for university. He was playing football on a scholarship in Eastern Canada. Peter would have been so proud! She went to most of the games and was sure she could feel Peter's presence there, a calm, warm, secure feeling. His spirit would be with her for the rest of her life. They were both free.

18

Summer 2018

What if you had listened? What if you had proceeded to follow the advice given to Peter and Samantha or if you had invested as Martha and Harvey? Let's see what happened.

Martha and Harvey had kept their three condominiums and one house in Toronto. Their monthly cash-flow after expenses was $13,000/month. They had worked to pay them off so that had no mortgages. The properties had a combined value of just over 3.2 million dollars. That meant that their cap rate – or return on that 3.2 million dollar investment – was 4.8%. Harvey and Martha were concerned, however. Should prices drop, they would be taking a significant hit on their net worth. On the other hand, the cash flow they were receiving meant that they didn't have to worry about anything financially. Should they hold the properties or sell them?

They had heard that properties in other parts of Canada were returning from 6%-10% after expenses (not counting mortgage costs). If they were able to find such investments, their monthly cash flow would be in the range of $25,000. They decided to start selling their Toronto Properties and look for those opportunities.

The first step was to talk to their accountant. They were on their fourth firm in 10 years. When they would start with an accounting practice things would go along quite well, but usually after the second year fees would double or even triple for advice and tax preparation services. When they would ask for a detailed itemized bill so that they could understand what was going on, generally they were told that their business was no longer something the firms wanted to help with.

Harvey was furious, wanting to report all of them to their regulatory body. Martha simply shook her head, negotiated the bills down and started looking for the next firm. They found a one-woman practice that seemed to be working out, but after all it was only the first year.

When they talked to their accountant they were told that they would be paying capital gains tax of over 1 million dollars because they had to add in all of the depreciation they had deducted over the years. After some thinking they decided to bite the bullet, sell the properties and pay the taxes. It was time to take those profits.

Samantha has also realized a significant increase in the value of her properties over the 10 years. Samantha knew that if she sold all of her seven buildings her gain on the properties would be over 1.5 million and a total cash infusion of 2.56 million dollars after taxes. They were properties primarily purchased in the Toronto region and the prices there had gone through the roof. There were no more mortgages on those properties.

Samantha's friends would often say that she was just plain lucky. She had read the book "fooled by randomness" so she fully understood what they were saying. The difference between what her friends were saying and what Samantha did was that she acted on her beliefs and business sense. Of course a great deal was random luck. But she had to be "in the game" to realize that good fortune. She didn't feel one bit of guilt for her success but decided after a coffee with Martha and Harvey to also sell her properties as well. It was time to take a profit.

Once the dust had cleared, Martha and Harvey had $2,155,432 in the bank with all taxes and fees paid. Samantha was sitting on $2,432,000 as she had to pay a bit more in taxes than she had originally thought. What should they do now?

19

Looking to Other Provinces

Martha, Harvey and Samantha decided to take a road trip to look for their next investments. They had reviewed many cities in Canada where they thought they could receive a better return on their investments and also thought it would be fun to catch up.

Their first stop – Halifax, Nova Scotia – happened to also be their last stop.

Their goal was to invest $700,000 in investment grade real estate. After that they were going to begin investing in other alternate forms of assets such as stocks, bonds, private lending opportunities and even venture fund investing.

In Nova Scotia they learned that:

1.   Landlords have rights, not just tenants. Very different from what is happening in Ontario;
2.   Prices in Nova Scotia go up and down gradually, not a lot of upside but significant cash flow opportunity;
3.   Property taxes are reasonable. Unlike Ontario or New Brunswick where Municipal Governments seem to have lost their way;
4.   Outstanding property management. They stumbled upon a management firm www.treepad.ca (real company owned

by our son Joshua) that specializes in managing student rentals

5.   Limited supply. In most University towns it is difficult to build new buildings and many are of C- in quality. By providing high quality buildings they could lead the industry.

So together they purchased 1.4 million dollars in student properties in Halifax, Nova Scotia. They were A-B quality, meaning they needed little repairs, however all were charging rents less than market value. Six months after purchase the team had their properties fully rented with an 8% return once all costs were taken out, including management. They were realizing a cash flow of $112,000 and because of depreciation most of that was tax free. They were each making $56,000 and decided to meet annually in Nova Scotia during the lobster season to review their properties and evaluate future purchasing opportunities.

Back home they looked at dividing up their other profits. Here's what they decided (annual cash-flow in brackets):

Short Term GIC's investing $400,000 at 3.5% ($14,000)

Private Lending of First Mortgages of $400,000 at 8% ($32,000)

Dividend-Paying Stocks $300,000 ($15,000)

Alternative Energy $100,000 on their Nova Scotia properties to reverse meter power-14% return ($14,000)

Angel and Funding to Start-Ups $100,000 (0 long term investments not paying dividend)

Real Estate, the $700,000 purchased in Nova Scotia ($56,000)

Cash in a savings account for future investments: Samantha $432,000; Harvey and Martha $155,432

Pre-tax annual cash flow $131,000

Now let's look at the details of how they accomplished this.

20

GIC's

In Canada GIC's were paying from 3.5% for a one year to 3.7% for a five-year commitment when the team searched for the best rates at www.ratehub.ca Harvey wondered about the need for a government insurance plan on their investments that all Banks and some Credit Unions provided. They learned that if the money was not insured and if something happened to the Credit Union, for example, they could lose their investments. While the rates weren't as high as the Credit Unions they went and invested their money in a conventional one year GIC.

The difference between one and three years was minimal, and they wanted to have their funds available after the first year. The problem would be taxes. They learned that they would lose approximately half of their interest income to taxes each year. Nevertheless, it was about security knowing that whatever the stock market would do wouldn't impact their cash holdings that drew them to this very conservative investment vehicle.

Private Lending

Private Lending is a type of investment where Harvey, Samantha and Martha would act as a bank lending their funds to others to purchase property. A quick search of Private Lending rates online told Samantha they needed to add this to their investment portfolios as interest rates for Private Mortgages ranged from 8% to 14% or more.

They were concerned, however, that if the borrower wouldn't pay they would then need to foreclose on them which would require extensive legal and other costs.

To attempt to reduce their risk they set up a simple guide when deciding on how to lend.

1. The character and work ethic of the borrower was the most important. After the interview and review of all documents, how likely is this person to stop fighting to find a way to pay their mortgage payments? Are they likely to take on an extra job or even three extra jobs to make sure they meet their obligations? Do they have a strong history of working to overcome challenges? How much do they hate debt?

2. The quality of the home or investment property. Would they be pleased to own the property should the borrower default? When sold, would they get their money back?

3. Down payment. Was the borrower willing to put at least 10% down or in the opinion of the team was the purchase price so below market value that 100% or even 125% mortgage to the value of the building was a reasonably safe investment?

Based on these factors the team would decide if they were wanting to loan the money on the first mortgage and at what rate. Only first mortgages would be considered as they were the safest in comparison to second and third mortgages.

They also discovered a social lending platform www.lendingloop.ca On this site small business owners were searching out financing for a variety of projects. The platform vetted the borrowers rating them from an A-E on credit risk. It was also possible to lend as little as $25 per borrower, so the team was able to spread their loans out over 100's of borrowers to spread their risk. The goal was to invest from $10,000 to $20,000 per year with a targeted return of 11% on those funds.

Dividend-Paying Stocks

The team decided to focus on the stocks of businesses they understood. The first goal was to look at Canadian Real Estate Companies or REIT's. These companies held large apartment buildings in different parts of Canada. The second industry was something they understood because with aging parents they knew about the home-care industry. They wanted to invest in companies that were blazing the trail to provide better home care for seniors by using technology. Here are the companies they chose.

Real Estate (Dividend in Brackets)

Killam Apartments (4.06%) They started in Atlantic Canada but currently own apartments in most parts of Canada.

Boardwalk (2.05%) Primarily in Calgary and Western Canada this company also has expanded to Ontario. With strong leadership and prudent property management this exceptional company has been impacted by oil prices which don't do it justice.

Northview Apartments (6.52%) Started primarily in Northern Canada, this company has moved to property ownership through acquisitions across the country.

Northwest Healthcare (7.37%) This is a medical office/hospital landlord. In Canada they provide clinics to doctors and other health care providers. In Australia they provide similar types of office ownership which provides for diversification and strong growth.

Pure Multi Family (5.07%) This Canadian REIT owns high quality apartments in the United States, only in warmer climates where people want to retire.

Inovalis Real Estate Investment Trust (8.12%) This company owns office buildings in France and Germany. It provides for a strong dividend and diversification in holdings.

First National Financial Corporation (6.72%) Linked to the Real Estate Industry this lender provides first mortgages to small business owners who often are unable to achieve a loan from conventional banks. Strong growth and dedicated customers leads to this second tier real estate play.

Laurentian Bank (6.11%) This Bank was beaten up because a number of borrowers "fibbed" a bit on their mortgage applications. Primarily business owners and self-employed professionals, they initially were thought to be poor credit risks. Turns out they are paying their mortgages monthly without hesitation to a level better than those with salaries who were working for others who had verified incomes on their mortgage applications. Primarily in Quebec, this Bank is taking advantage of the booming economy and gradually the markets are understanding the under value of this great company.

Average return of 5.5% not including appreciation of stock price.

Virtual Care Stocks Paying no Dividends

These stocks were more junior in nature with no dividends paid. The goal was to find Canadian companies who were focused on Virtual Care of Seniors and others who may be ill, providing much needed vital care to their homes.

Reliq Health Technologies Inc. This company provides services to American Patients who are able to leave the hospital earlier because of Reliq's technology. Reliq provides home monitoring and assistance to patients while communicating vital information to hospitals and physicians. (the team purchased Reliq stock for 13 cents and then sold the majority of their holdings for $2.30. They continue to hold some stock for long term growth.)

Protech Home Medical Corp. This Canadian company provides at-home services for medical and respiratory equipment.

Viemed Healthcare Inc. Provides services in home for respiratory care (spin off from Protech).

Nova Leap Health Corporation provides traditional in-home care services primarily to seniors. Acting as an employment agency, the company places workers in clients' homes, earning their revenue from the private pay for these services by residents.

Alternative Energy (14% return)

In Ontario the Green Energy Act of 2009 was a once-in-a-life-time opportunity for some investors. Harvey and Martha knew of some of their friends who purchased solar panels for their small farms and sold the electricity back into the grid for 80 cents per KWH. But people in Ontario at that time were only paying 8 or 9 cents per KWH. How did this make any sense?

The cost of solar panels and other components needed to make those systems in 2009 resulted in a return of approximately 14%. So a $100,000 unit was producing approximately $14,000 in cash each year with the contract extended for 20 years.

In 2018, the cost of the solar panels and other equipment had dropped drastically. While the Green Energy Act was discontinued by the next Provincial Government, a new opportunity appeared. Reverse Metering. This allowed a home owner or business to put up solar panels and, when power was produced, the meter on the property went in reverse to credit the use to the home owner. Because prices had dropped so significantly a $15,000 investment in a unit to reverse meter all of the power needs of a small office building resulted in a savings of $2,100 per year, or a return of 14% on that investment. In Nova Scotia a similar program exists, so the team decided to reverse meter all of their buildings and charge tenants a flat rate for their hydro use. This resulted in a return of 15%-18% per building. The contracts to reverse meter were guaranteed with no limiting time to them. In essence they were becoming their own utility company with minimal risk.

Angel Funding and Start-ups

The team remembered when they were starting out in their investment careers how they were helped along the way. Banks were becoming tougher on new startups and young people who wanted to purchase new equipment or services to expand their business. Intrigued by the link of technology to home care and other such investments, they began the long journey of understanding Angel and Start-up investing.

They began by signing up at www.frontfundr.com a service that reviews different start-up proposals for equity funding and investment opportunities for investors who understand the risk. The understanding is that most ventures will fail or barely survive while 1-2 in 10 will provide a reasonable return. These are high risk investments and anyone in this game must understand they could lose all of their money. As a result, $50,000 was the most each would put into these investments. It was great fun and when they had finished their first "round" of investing each had 10 companies in their portfolios. From a vegan butcher to remote vital sign monitoring sent directly to cardiologists, they were excited about the prospects. They also realized that it could take from 5-10 years before they would realize any return on their investments. It was going to be a lot of fun.

Investments They Avoided

Harvey, Martha and Samantha were constantly bombarded with new investment ideas from friends and family. The trend of investing in "pot" stocks, cryptocurrency or exotic real estate investments were avoided like the plague. One acquaintance even suggested they buy exotic time shares across the country. All were quickly declined.

One bank manager suggested Mutual Funds so that they could sleep at night and not have to work so hard managing their money. The team then learned of the commissions of up to 3% for some funds and other costs that made them nervous. ETF's were also avoided. Too general and too much like a flock of sheep following a weak leader.

Yes it was work to manage their own money and learn about the different investment options. It was taking about 5-6 hours a week to review all quarterly statements, review information with their property managers or talk together as a team on a Skype call about next steps. But this investment philosophy was about diversification and smart investing. They were well on their way. But now that the money was taken care of what should be their new priorities for life?

Giving Back

They felt very lucky and fortunate. They could plan and spend their days as they wished. They had monthly income of just over $10,000, most of it tax free. They had diversity of investments so that if one got in trouble they still would be fine. They had cash in the bank to take care of emergencies or new investment opportunities. They each were spending only $4,000/month on all living expenses and luxuries so they were still saving over $70,000/year. Being in their situation, however, motivated them to look at how to give back to their communities and others less fortunate.

Martha was concerned as she had learned of fraud and theft from a non-profit she supported to the tune of 2.8 million dollars. Many other charities were using a significant amount of donations for administration or other overhead with little money actually going to the intended cause. This is why they decided to give back through www.kiva.org an organization that provides interest free loans to entrepreneurs around the world, primarily in impoverished countries. They each agreed to put $10,000 into the fund. The money would be loaned out at 0% interest to these businesses, once returned to be loaned out again. Each year they would consider adding to their contributions. It was painless, fit with their philosophy of helping but requiring responsibility and care of the funds by those receiving. It was a good fit.

Harvey and Martha also wanted to give back by mentoring other young adults or business owners. Many were asking them but they wanted to focus on those with a strong work ethic and passion for business.

Finding Chi

Harvey and Martha were finishing their annual winter trip to Florida. While lounging by the pool with their luggage for a final few moments of sun, they learned that their flight had been cancelled due to freezing rain at the Toronto Airport. There was no indication of any flight back home for a couple of days. So Harvey sat back in the lounge chair and began to watch the clouds. Nothing I can do anyway, he thought. Might as well enjoy this weather.

Martha continued reading her book. It seemed like only a few moments had passed but it turned out that Harvey was watching the clouds for over three hours. When finally alerted back to reality something had happened. It was as if he were filled with incredible joy, freedom from any worry or concern, a deep sense of being within the moment and fully alert to the sounds, smells and other senses that were firing on overload. It was very strange. Martha was very concerned about how and when to organize the flight home, but Harvey didn't care. It didn't matter. Nothing was as important as being in the moment, with the sun, the warm air, the sounds..........

It didn't change. Harvey thought that perhaps he had just had a deep relaxation moment and would quickly return to normal. But that didn't happen.

When they finally got back home, Harvey contacted a friend who, when he heard the story, quickly stated "You found chi". Harvey didn't know he was looking for it. In Japan they call it Ki, in India Prana, and in China Chi. Most cultures identify this very important life force.

Harvey was still confused. How could staring at clouds by a pool in Florida for a few hours after his plane got cancelled create this incredible, life-altering experience?

The answer is there is no answer. It's something Harvey had to accept and enjoy. He just hoped his friends, family and especially Martha could find Chi.

21

Millennials-Money Habits and

the FIRE Movement

Harvey wondered about the advice to provide a young income earner today. How could he help them achieve his sense of control over his/her financial life?

The FIRE movement (Financial Independence Retire Early) is certainly popular today. Mr. Money Mustache http://www.mrmoneymustache.com/ and hundreds of others continue to advise young earners on how to save and scrimp so that they can retire before the age of 40 or even 35.

It was an important question as Harvey was about to mentor his next young business owner over coffee the next day. He decided to write down what he would do if starting today. Here's his list.

1. Save between 10% and 40% of income. Have that amount taken off automatically each pay period. If you are working full-time and living with parents you MUST save 90% of your salary for future investments.
2. Place those funds in a high interest, government guaranteed savings account.

3. When $10,000 or more is available, invest in a small duplex, living in one renting out the other.
4. Move to an area where the cost of living is reasonable.
5. Separate wants from needs. Focus on needs 99% of the time.
6. Never borrow money to buy a depreciating toy that has no value. i.e. car
7. Give back to others. Don't wait until you are financially strong, do this from day one.
8. Avoid toxic people and relationships.
9. Seek out a mentor that has achieved or been successful. Someone who is where you want to be.
10. Begin investing in Public companies that pay a strong dividend. Do this within a TFSA.
11. Exercise at least five times a week. People who engage in regular exercise are more successful in all other aspects of life.
12. Eat Healthy food. Are you? If you want to know how you are doing go to the Apple or Google app store and download Click-Eat the healthy diet and a registered Dietitian will let you know.
13. Take steps to find CHI. More time to self-reflect and meditate with no purpose.
14. Read at least one book per month on finance, real estate or any other area of self-improvement interest.
15. Love

Be well and I look forward to writing the next update in 2028. (To get regular money and investment advice with updates subscribe to the "Shrink Money Advice Podcast" at www.awesound.com and go to the Shrink Money Advice Facebook Page.

Henry

www.ingramcontent.com/pod-product-compliance
Lightning Source LLC
Chambersburg PA
CBHW020929180526
45163CB00007B/2937